The Information Lens, an Intelligent System for Information Sharing in Organizations

The Information Lens:
An Intelligent System for
Information Sharing in Organizations

Thomas W. Malone
Kenneth R. Grant
Franklyn A. Turbank

January 1986

CISR WP No. 133
Sloan WP No. 1749-86
90s WP No. 86-016

Center for Information Systems Research

Massachusetts Institute of Technology
Sloan School of Management
77 Massachusetts Avenue
Cambridge, Massachusetts, 02139

The Information Lens: An Intelligent System for Information Sharing in Organizations

Thomas W. Malone
Kenneth R. Grant
Franklyn A. Turbank

January 1986

CISR WP No. 133
Sloan WP No 1749-86
90s WP No 86-016

This paper will appear in the Proceedings of the CHI '86 Conference on Human Factors in Computing Systems (sponsored by ACM/SIGCHI), Boston, Mass, April 1986

CENTER FOR INFORMATION SYSTEMS RESEARCH
Sloan School of Management
Massachusetts Institute of Technology

Abstract

This paper describes an intelligent system to help people share and filter information communicated by computer-based messaging systems The system exploits concepts from artificial intelligence such as frames, production rules, and inheritance networks, but it avoids the unsolved problems of natural language understanding by providing users with a rich set of semi-structured message templates A consistent set of "direct manipulation" editors simplifies the use of the system by individuals, and an incremental enhancement path simplifies the adoption of the system by groups

.

The Information Lens:
An Intelligent System for Information Sharing in Organizations

One of the key problems that arises when any group of people cooperates to solve problems or make decisions is how to share information Thus one of the central goals of designing good "organizational interfaces" (Malone, 1985) should be to help people share information in groups and organizations In this paper, we will describe a prototype system, called the Information Lens, that focuses on one aspect of this problem how to help people share the many diverse kinds of qualitative information that are communicated via electronic messaging systems

It is already a common experience in mature computer-based messaging communities for people to feel flooded with large quantities of electronic "junk mail" (Denning, 1982, Palme, 1984, Wilson, 1984, Hiltz & Turoff, 1985), and the widespread availability of inexpensive communication capability has the potential to overwhelm people with even more messages that are of little or no value to them At the same time, it is also a common experience for people to be ignorant of facts that would facilitate their work and that are known elsewhere in their organization The system we will describe helps solve both these problems it helps people filter, sort, and prioritize messages that are already addressed to them, and it also helps them find useful messages they would not otherwise have received

The most common previous approach to structuring information sharing in electronic messaging environments is to let users implicitly specify their general areas of interest by associating themselves with centralized distribution lists or conference topics related to particular subjects (e g , Hiltz & Turoff, 1978) Since these methods of disseminating information are often targeted for relatively large audiences, however, it is usually impossible for all the information distributed to be of interest to all recipients

The Information Lens system uses much more detailed representations of message contents and receivers' interests to provide more sophisticated filtering possibilities One of the key ideas behind this system is that many of the unsolved problems of natural language understanding can be avoided by using semi-structured templates (or frames) for different types of messages These templates are used by the senders of messages to facilitate composing messages in the first place Then, the same templates are used by the receivers of messages to facilitate constructing a set of rules to be used for filtering and categorizing messages of different types

Background Studies of information sharing in organizations To help understand the kinds of automated aids for sharing information that would be desirable, we conducted several preliminary studies of how various kinds of information are shared in organizations These studies are described in more detail elsewhere (Brobst, Malone, Grant, & Cohen, 1985) They included interviews of over 50 people about their information filtering experiences, needs, and desires in different kinds of situations such as processing the contents of their in-boxes and reading their electronic mail In each case, we asked the subjects to explain in detail why they made the filtering decisions they did Then we used these "expert protocols" to identify the general processes and specific kinds of knowledge that people used for extracting information from a large pool of available sources As noted below, the insights from these studies are reflected in our system

Key ideas

There are five key ideas that, together, form the basis of the Information Lens system Though some of these ideas are empirically testable hypotheses, we treat them here as premises for our system design We will list and briefly describe these ideas here In the next sections, we will describe in more detail how the Lens system uses them

(1) *A rich set of semi-structured message types (or frames) can form the basis for an intelligent information sharing system* For example, meeting announcements can be structured as templates that include fields for "time", "place", "organizer", and "topic", as well as any additional unstructured information There are three reasons why this idea is important

    (a) *Semi-structured messages enable computers to automatically process a much wider range of information than would otherwise be possible* By letting people compose messages that already have much of their essential information structured in fields, we eliminate the need for any kind of automatic parsing or understanding of free text messages while still representing enough information to allow quite sophisticated rules to process the messages

    (b) *Much of the processing people already do with the information they receive reflects a set of semi-structured message types* In our informal studies we found that people often described their filtering heuristics according to categories of documents being filtered (e g , *This is a brochure advertising a seminar I usually throw these away unless the title intrigues me or unless it looks like a brochure I could use as a model for the ones I write* -- paraphrased comments of a research center administrator in the in-box study)

    (c) *Even if no automatic processing of messages were involved, providing a set of semi-structured message templates to the authors of messages would often be helpful* Two of the people in our informal interviews mentioned simple examples of this phenomenon one remarked about how helpful it would be if any memo requesting some kind of action included, in a prominent place, the deadline by which the action needed to be taken, a second commented about how wonderful it would be if all the meeting invitations he received included a field about why he was supposed to be there We will see below how message templates can be provided in a flexible way that encourages, but does not require, their use

(2) *Sets of production rules (that may include multiple levels of reasoning, not just Boolean selection criteria) can be used to conveniently specify automatic processing for these messages*

(3) *The use of semi-structured message types and automatic rules for processing them can be greatly simplified by a consistent set of display-oriented editors for composing messages, constructing rules, and defining new message templates*

(4) *The definition and use of semi-structured messages and processing rules are simplified if the message types are arranged in a frame inheritance lattice*

(5) *The initial introduction and later evolution of a group communication system can be much easier if the process can occur as a series of small changes, each of which has the following properties (a) individual users can continue to use their existing system with no change if they so desire, (b) individual users who make small changes receive some immediate benefit, and (c) groups of users who adopt the changes receive additional benefits beyond the individual benefits*

System overview

In order to provide a natural integration of this system with the capabilities that people already use, our system is built on top of an existing electronic mail system Users can continue to send and receive their mail as usual In addition, the Lens system provides four important optional capabilities (1) People can use structured message templates to help them compose and read their messages, (2) Receivers can specify rules to automatically filter and classify messages arriving in their mailbox, (3) Senders can include as an addressee of a message, in addition to specific individuals or distribution lists, a special mailbox (currently named "LENS") to indicate that the sender is willing to have this message automatically redistributed to anyone else who might be interested, and (4) Receivers can specify rules that find and show messages addressed to LENS that the receiver would not otherwise have seen

By gradually adding new message types and new rules, users can continually increase the helpfulness of the system without ever being dependent on its ability to perfectly filter all messages

System architecture The Lens system is being developed in the Interlisp-D programming environment using Loops, an object-oriented extension of Lisp The system runs on Xerox 1108 processors connected by an Ethernet We use parts of the Lafite mail system and the XNS network protocols already provided in that environment The message construction aids and the individual filtering rules all operate on the users' personal workstations

As Figure 1 illustrates, messages that include LENS as an addressee will be delivered by the existing mail server directly to the explicit addressees as well as to an automatic mail sorter that runs on a workstation and periodically retrieves messages from the special mailbox This automatic mail sorter may then in turn, send the message to several additional recipients whose rules selected it (In our test version of the system, we expect to achieve the same functionality with somewhat slower performance by having LENS be a distribution list including all recipients participating in the system test All the messages addressed to LENS will be automatically screened at the recipient's workstation, and those that pass the tests a recipient has specified will be shown to that recipient)

Implementation status The Information Lens system as described in this paper currently exists in early prototype form Except where noted, all the features described below have been implemented and received limited internal testing As of this writing, the system has been in regular use by the members of our research group for about one month Additional system integration, hardening, and extension efforts are currently underway

Messages

The Lens system is based on a set of semi-structured messages For each message type, the system includes a template with a number of fields or slots for holding information Associated with each field are several properties, including the default value of the field, a list of likely alternative values for the field, and an explanation of why the field is part of the template

Figures 2 and 3 show a sample of the highly graphical interaction through which users can construct messages using these templates (see Tou, Williams, Fikes, Henderson & Malone, 1982, for a similar approach to constructing database retrieval queries) After selecting a field of a message by pointing with a mouse, the user can point with the mouse again to see the field's default value, an explanation of the field's purpose, or a list of likely alternatives for filling in the field If the user selects one of these alternatives, that value is automatically inserted in the message text The user can also edit any fields directly at any time using the built-in display-oriented text editor For example, the user can add as much free text as desired in the text field of the message

Information LENS

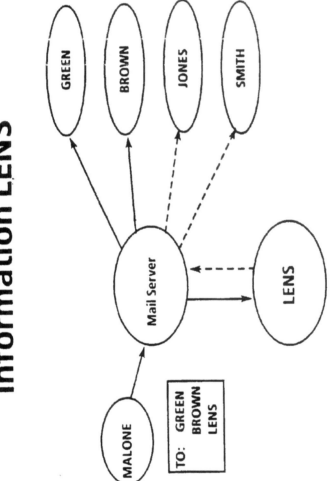

Figure 1

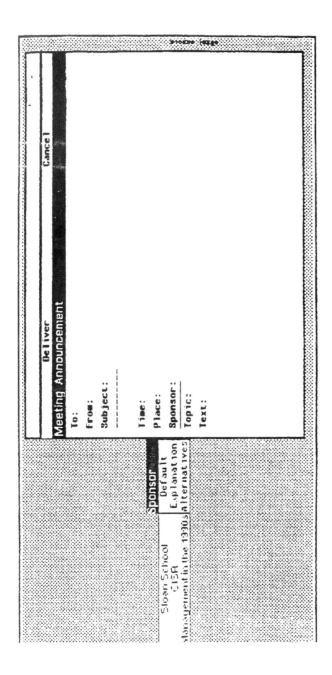

Figure 2

8

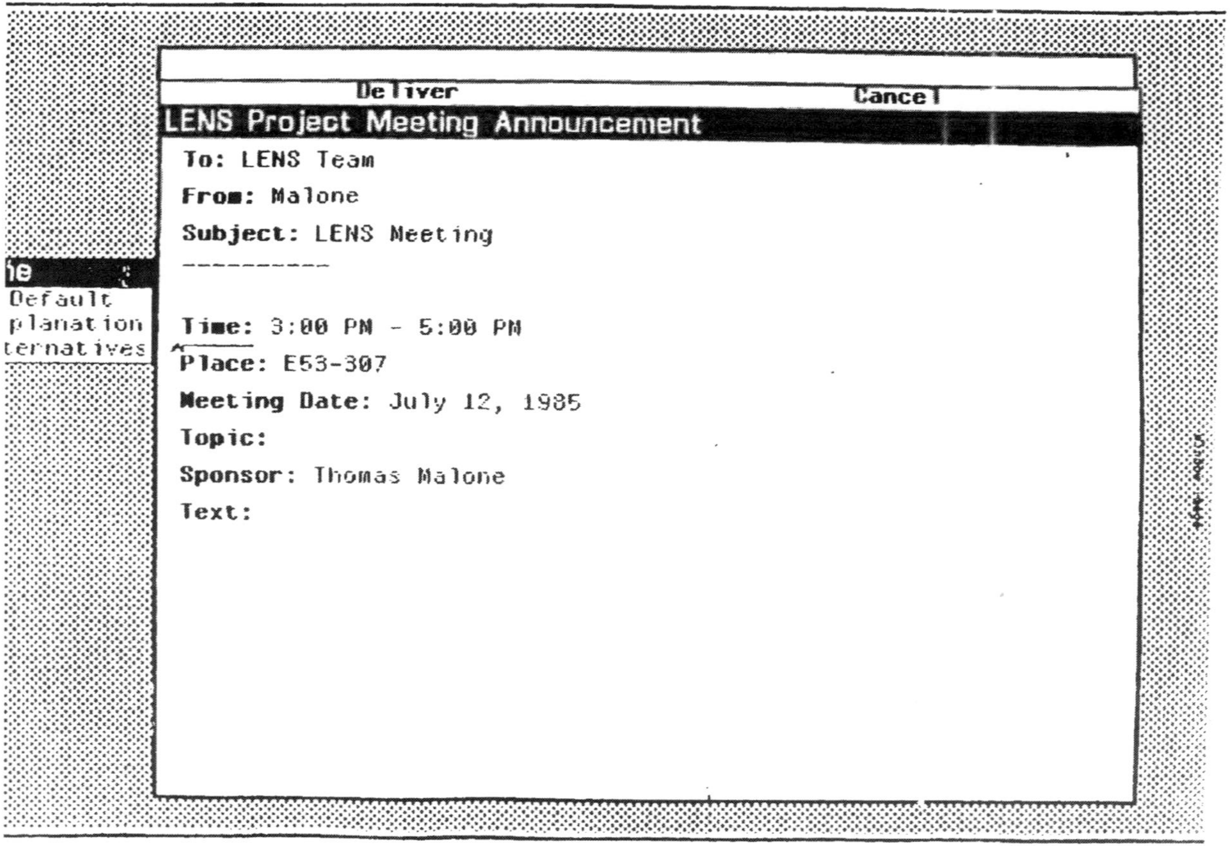

9

Deliver   Cancel

LENS Project Meeting Announcement

To: LENS Team

From: Malone

Subject: LENS Meeting

Time: 3:00 PM - 5:00 PM

Place: E53-307

Meeting Date: July 12, 1985

Topic:

Sponsor: Thomas Malone

Text:

Default
planation
ternatives

By providing a wealth of domain-specific knowledge about the default and alternative values for particular types of messages, the system can make the construction of some messages much easier For example, Figure 3 shows how some message templates, such as a regular weekly meeting announcement, may have default values already filled in for most of their fields and require only a few keystrokes or mouse clicks to complete and send off

Users who do not want to take advantage of these message construction aids can simply select the most general message type (*message*) and use the text editor to fill in the standard fields (To, From, and Subject) just as they would have done in the previous mail system We expect, however, that the added convenience provided to the senders by semi-structured templates will be a significant incentive for senders to use templates in constructing some of their messages This, in turn, will greatly increase the amount of information receivers can use in constructing automatic processing rules for incoming messages

Direct manipulation Both the message editor and the rule editor (described below) embody the features that Shneiderman (1982, p 251) uses to characterize "direct manipulation" interfaces "(1) continuous representation of the object of interest, (2) physical actions or labelled button presses instead of complex syntax, and (3) rapid incremental reversible operations whose impact on the object of interest is immediately visible " We believe that these features help explain the simplicity of using these editors

Message types

To further simplify the construction and use of message templates the templates are arranged in a network so that all subtypes of a given template *inherit* the field names and property values (e g , defaults, explanations, and alternatives) from the *parent* template Any subtype may, in turn, add new fields or override any of the property values inherited from the parent (e g , see Fikes & Kehler, 1985) For example, the *seminar announcement* template adds a field for *speaker* that is not present in its parent template *meeting announcement* The *LENS project meeting announcement* (Figure 3) adds a number of default values that are not present in its parent The inheritance network eliminates the need to continually re-enter redundant information when constructing new templates that resemble old ones, and it provides a natural way of organizing templates, thus making it easier for senders to select the right template

The message type lattice is made visible to the user through the message type browser Figure 4 shows this lattice browser for our sample network of message types Users select a template to use in

By clicking with a different mouse button, users can view or modify the rules (see below) associated with a particular message type Like the other message type characteristics, these rules are inherited by the subtypes of a message template

Group definition of message types The network shown in Figure 4 includes some message types that we believe will be useful in almost all organizations (e g , meeting announcements) and some that are important only in our environment (e g , LENS project meeting announcement) Different groups can develop detailed structures to represent the information of specific concern to them For example, a product design team might have an elaborate network of message types describing different aspects of the product (*e g* , market size estimates, response time estimates, alternative power supply vendors) Then, for instance, marketing specialists who believe that the critical factors determining potential market size for the product are cost and response time can devote most of their attention to the messages concerning these factors and ignore all the rest of the technical specifications for the product

We are developing another display-oriented editor, like the message editor shown in Figures 2 and 3, for creating and modifying the template definitions themselves We expect that in some (e g , rarely used) regions of the network anyone should be able to use this "template editor" to modify an existing message type or define a new one, while in other regions, only specifically designated people should have access to this capability In the current version of the system people can use a simple version of this editor to personalize the *default, explanation*, and *alternatives* properties of the fields in existing message types

A given user's *personal profile* consists of these customizations of the message types, together with a set of personal rules for processing messages (see next section), and a set of hierarchically arranged folders in which messages can be stored

Message purpose One characteristic of message classes that is critical in formulating filtering rules is the *purpose* of the message We expect that an important part of the frame inheritance network for message types will be a taxonomy of the various *communication acts* that a message might embody (e g , Searle, 1975, Kedzierski, 1984) For example, messages whose purpose is to *request information* should be routed to people who know about the topic of the message, while messages whose purpose is to *provide information* should be routed to people who are interested in the topic of the message

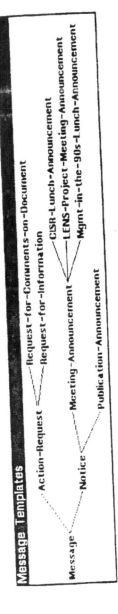

Message Templates

Message
  Action-Request
    Request-for-Comments-on-Document
    Request-for-Information
  Notice
    Meeting-Announcement
      CISR-Lunch-Announcement
      LENS-Project-Meeting-Announcement
      Mgmt-in-the-90s-Lunch-Announcement
    Publication-Announcement

Figure 4

Rules

The Lens environment allows users to build rules for finding, filtering, and sorting messages. Rules consist of a test and an action, if a message satisfies the test, then the action specified by the rule is performed on the message

Figures 5 through 9 show examples of the display-oriented editor used to construct rules. This editor uses rule templates that are based on the same message types as those used for message construction. We expect that this template-based graphical rule construction will be much easier for inexperienced computer users than more conventional rule or query languages

Constructing the "IF" part of a rule involves filling in selection specifications for the different fields of the message. The simplest kind of selection specification is a string that should appear somewhere in the specified field. More complex specifications for a field can be constructed by combining strings with *and, or, not,* and parentheses (i e , arbitrary boolean combinations are possible within a field). If specifications appear in more than one field, then all specifications must be satisfied at once for the rule to succeed (i e , specifications in different fields are implicitly *and*-ed). As in the message editor, the default, alternatives, and explanation menus are available in the rule editor, here they facilitate the construction of selection specifications. To specify the action ("THEN" part) of a rule, users select the word "THEN" on the rule template and then choose an action from the menu of possibilities that appears. Typical actions classify messages in specific folders (Figure 5) or delete messages (Figure 6)

As mentioned above, rules can also be used to find messages of interest that are addressed to "LENS" but which a particular user would not otherwise have seen. Figure 7 is an example of such a rule. The *show* option for the action of a rule indicates that the central mail sorter should forward messages that satisfy the rule test to the person who constructed the rule

Message characteristics In our informal studies of people filtering information, we observed many instances of what could be modeled as a kind of multi-level processing in the first phase, items were classified (e g , "This message is from someone I don't know " or "This article sounds too OR-ish ") and then, in the second phase, some action was taken (e g , " so I will throw it away") A production rule formalism like we are using is, of course, well suited for representing this kind of multi-level reasoning We capture a simple form of it by including in every rule template, in addition to the fields associated with the message type, a field for *characteristics* Certain rules set the characteristics of messages, based on other field values, and then other rules can test messages for these characteristics For example, Figures 8 and 9 show how we can construct a single rule that determines whether a message is from a VIP and then test for this characteristic in other rules This

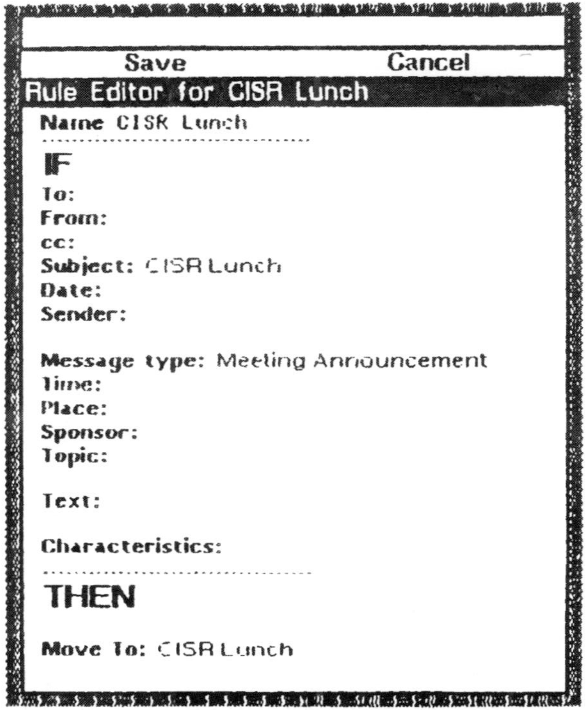

| Save | Cancel |

Rule Editor for CISR Lunch

Name CISR Lunch

IF

To:
From:
cc:
Subject: CISR Lunch
Date:
Sender:

Message type: Meeting Announcement
Time:
Place:
Sponsor:
Topic:

Text:

Characteristics:

THEN

Move To: CISR Lunch

Figure 5

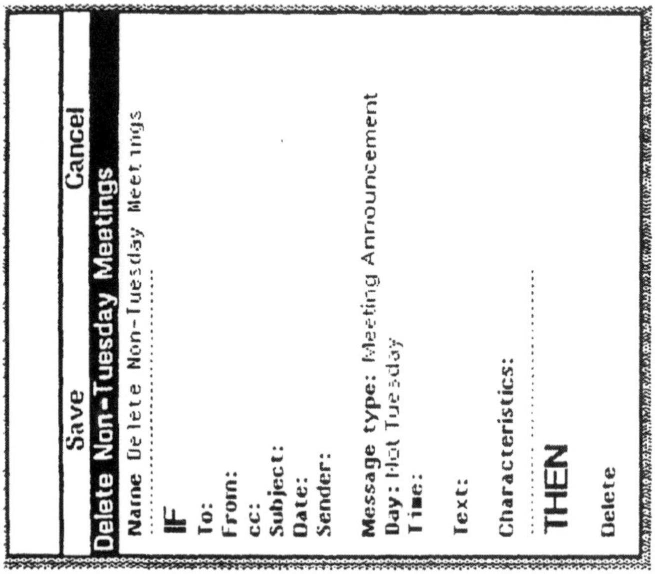

Save	Cancel

Delete Non-Tuesday Meetings

Name Delete Non-Tuesday Meetings

IF

To:

From:

cc:

Subject:

Date:

Sender:

Message type: Meeting Announcement

Day: Not Tuesday

Time:

Text:

Characteristics:

THEN

Delete

Figure 6

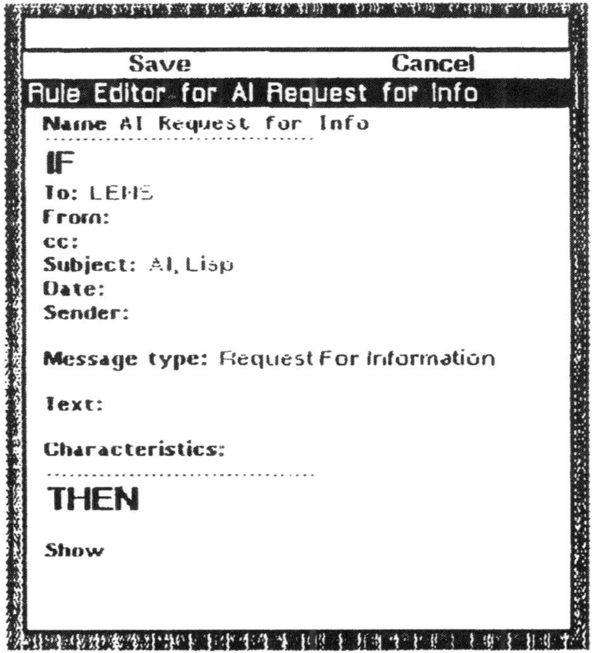

Save   **Cancel**

Rule Editor for AI Request for Info

Name AI Request for Info

IF

To: LENS
From:
cc:
Subject: AI, Lisp
Date:
Sender:

Message type: RequestFor Information

Text:

Characteristics:

THEN

Show

Figure 7

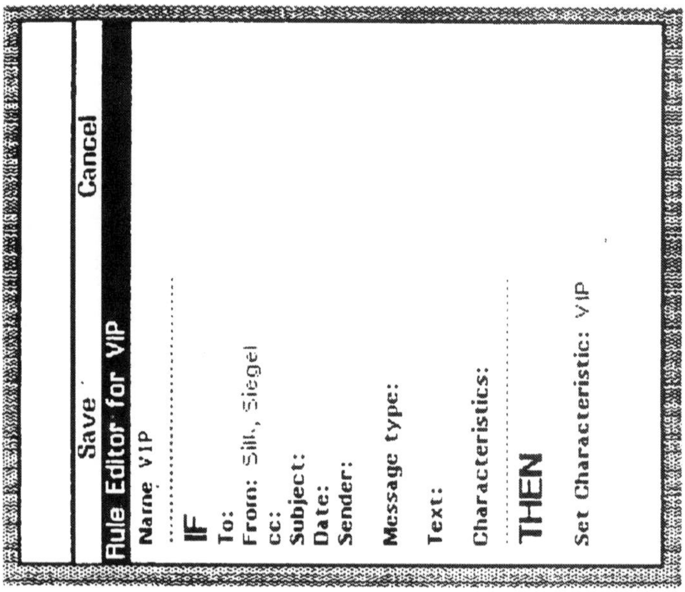

Save	Cancel

Rule Editor for VIP

Name VIP

IF

To:
From: Sill, Siegel
cc:
Subject:
Date:
Sender:

Message type:

Text:

Characteristics:

THEN

Set Characteristic: VIP

Figure 8

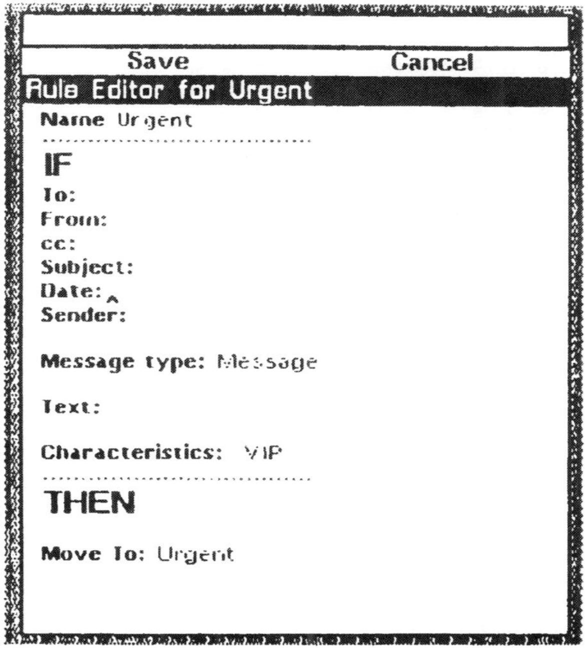

Rule Editor for Urgent

| Save | Cancel |

Name Urgent

IF

To:
From:
cc:
Subject:
Date: A
Sender:

Message type: Message

Text:

Characteristics: VIP

THEN

Move To: Urgent

Figure 9

kind of abstraction mechanism has obvious advantages over a mechanism that requires repeating the specifications of a VIP in all the rules that need to test for this characteristic Although specifications in different fields are implicitly "and"-ed, the characteristics mechanism also makes it possible to construct tests that include any combination of features in any combination of fields (i e , arbitrary boolean combinations between fields)

Group use of message types Individuals who begin using this system before most other people do can get some immediate benefit from constructing rules using only the fields present in all messages (To, From, Subject, Date) Groups of individuals who begin to use a set of common message types can get much greater benefits from constructing more sophisticated rules for dealing with more specialized message types For example, a general rule might try to recognize "bug reports" based on the word "bug" in the subject field, but this would be a very fallible test A community that uses a common template for bug reports can construct rules that deal only with messages the senders classify as bug reports These rules can use specialized information present in the template such as the system in which the bug occurred, the urgency of the request for repair, and so forth

Future Directions

One obvious and important extension to our system is to add a common *topic network* (similar to the network of message types that already exists) to let senders indicate the topic(s) of a message and let receivers filter on this basis Another extension we would like to explore involves adding a *knowledge-base server* which will keep copies of public messages Just as in a computer conferencing system, users will then be able to retrieve these messages at a later time even if they did not receive the messages originally

A related research direction involves integration of Lens with other on-line sources of knowledge Significant power can be added to the system by viewing field values as database objects rather than mere text strings Rules can then access information from these *embedded objects* in deciding how to handle messages For example, rules could check the job title or organizational position of the message sender if these characteristics were stored in a central database

One of the attractive features about the general system architecture we are using is that it is relatively easy to gradually add more and more kinds of knowledge For example, we would also like to experiment with having the system automatically reply or otherwise respond to certain kinds of messages (e g , meeting requests, purchase requisitions, etc)

Other approaches to information filtering We also intend to experiment with other approaches to the information filtering process itself The primary approach we have described so far might be called a *cognitive filtering* approach since it relies on characterizing the information contents of a message and the information needs of potential message recipients Even though the system depends on its human users to encode and interpret this information, the success of the system still relies on the ability of the message templates and rule templates to represent the information being communicated There are at least two other approaches to information filtering that do not require the system to represent the content of the messages at all (see Brobst et al [1985] for more detail)

(1) *Social filtering* supports the personal and organizational relationships among individuals in the electronic messaging community One simple example of this process that is already possible in our system is to filter a message based on characteristics of the sender (e g , messages from one's boss are high priority). A more elaborate example involves using endorsements For instance, the priority of a message for a given receiver could depend on the number of people whose opinions the receiver respected who had endorsed the message

(2) *Economic filtering* uses various kinds of positive and negative incentives to control the quantity and quality of information flows For example, just as people now often use 'bulk rate" postage as an indication of the (low) value of paper mail they receive, future message systems may let senders divide a fixed weekly budget of points among all their outgoing messages to indicate the importance of the messages Then receivers can use these point values, possibly together with characteristics of the sender, to filter incoming messages

Related work

There are several other previous approaches to structuring information sharing in electronic communities that have been used much less widely than distribution lists and conference topics These include (1) keyword filtering (e g , Stallman, 1983) and other techniques developed for large text retrieval systems (e g , Salton, 1983), and (2) using associative links between textual items to represent relationships such as references to earlier (or later) documents on similar topics, replies to previous messages, or examples of general concepts (e g , Engelbart, 1968, Trigg, 1983)

We have not focused here on facilitating the kind of real-time information sharing that occurs in face-to-face meetings (e g , Stefik et al, 1985 Sarin & Greif, 1984) or teleconferencing (e g , Johansen, 1984) We believe, however, that the aids we described could be useful in some real-time meetings (especially those involving very many people), and, more importantly, that these aids could eliminate the need for some meetings altogether

Conclusion

In this paper, we have described an intelligent system for supporting information sharing in organizations. The system appears to derive its power and simplicity from an unusual combination of ideas drawn from artificial intelligence, user interface design, and organizational science. We believe this system provides a prototypical example of how computer systems can be designed to include not only good *user interfaces* for supporting the problem solving of individuals, but also good *organizational interfaces* (Malone, 1985) for supporting the problem solving of groups of people.

Acknowledgments

This research was supported, in part, by Citibank, N A , by an equipment grant from the Xerox Corporation, by the Management in the 1990's Research Program at the Sloan School of Management, MIT, and by the Center for Information Systems Research, MIT Many of the original ideas for the Information Lens arose in conversations with Michael Cohen

References

Blair, D and Maron, M An evaluation of retrieval effectiveness for a full-text document-retrieval system *Communications of the ACM*, 28, 3, 1985 pp 289-299

Brobst, S A , Malone, T W , Grant, K R , & Cohen, M D , Toward intelligent message routing systems *Proceedings of the Second International Symposium on Computer Message Systems*, Washington, D C , September 5 - 7, 1985

Crawford, A Corporate electronic mail - A communication intensive application of information technology *MIS Quarterly*, September 1982, pp 1-14

Denning, P. Electronic junk · *Communications of the ACM*, 23, 3, 1982 pp 163-165

Englebart, D C and English, W K Research center for augmenting human intellect *Proceedings of Fall Joint Computing Congress*, AFIPS press, December 1968, pp 395-410

Fikes, R and Kehler, T. The role of frame-based representation in reasoning *Communications of the ACM*, 28, 7, 1985, p 904

Hiltz, S R and Turoff, M *The network nation   human communication via computer* Reading, Mass Addison-Wesley, 1978

Hiltz, S R and Turoff, M Structuring computer-mediated communication systems to avoid information overload *Communications of the ACM*, 28, 7, 1985, pp 680-689

Johansen, R *Teleconferencing and beyond Communications in the office of the future* New York McGraw-Hill, 1984

Kedzierski, B Knowledge-based project management and communication support in a system development environment *Fourth Jerusalem Conference on Information Technology* Jerusalem, Israel, 1984

Malone, T Designing organizational interfaces *Proceedings of the CHI '85 Conference on Human Factors in Computing Systems* San Francisco, California, 1985

Palme, J You have 134 unread mail do you want to read them now? *IFIP Conference on Computer Based Message Services* Nottingham University, 1984

Salton, G and McGill, M *Introduction to modern information retrieval* New York McGraw-Hill, 1983

Sarin, S K and Greif, I Interactive on-line conferences *Proceedings ACM-SIGOA Conference on Office Information Systems*, June 1984

Searle, J A taxonomy of illocutionary acts in K Gunderson (ed), *Minnesota Studies in the Philosophy of Language* Minneapolis University of Minnesota Press, 1975

Shneiderman, B   The future of interactive systems and the emergence of direct manipulation " *Behavior and Information Technology*, 1, 237-256, 1982

Shneiderman, B   Direct manipulation   A step beyond programming languages " *IEEE Computer*, 16, 57-69, August 1983

Stallman, R *ZMail manual* M I T Artificial Intelligence Laboratory, 1983

Stefik, M , Foster, G , Bobrow, D , Kahn, K , Lanning, S and Suchman, L *Beyond the chalkboard using computers to support collaboration and problem solving in meetings*   Intelligent Systems Laboratory Technical Report, Xerox Palo Alto Research Center, Palo Alto, CA, September, 1985

Tou, F N , Williams, M D , Fikes, R E , Henderson, D A , & Malone, T W RABBIT An intelligent daytabase assistant *Proceedings of the National Conference of the American Association for Artificial Intelligence*, Pittsburgh, Pennsylvania, August 18-20, 1982

Trigg, R *Network approach to text handling for the online scientific community* Ph D thesis, Department of Computer Science, University of Maryland, CSTR-1346, November 1983

Turoff, M *Information, value and the internal marketplace* New Jersey Institute of Technology, Newark, New Jersey, 1983

Wilson, P , Maude, T , Marshall, C , and Heaton, N The active mailbox - your on-line secretary *IFIP Conference on Computer Based Message Services* Nottingham University, 1984

Lightning Source UK Ltd.
Milton Keynes UK
UKHW020646190421
382245UK00006B/476